Women Who Were Warned

LindaAnn LoSchiavo

Cerasus Poetry
London N22 6LY

cerasuspoetry.com

High in the heavens I saw the moon this morning,
      Albeit the sun shone bright;
Unto my soul it spoke, in voice of warning,
      "Remember Night!"

"Warning" by Ella Wheeler Wilcox, 1910

CONTENTS

Cassandra's Curse

A tot, still inside a carriage, I
Unwittingly observed a sudden death.
In babytalk, I tried explaining: *truck,
Boom, bye-bye.* Pointing to my doll, I screamed,
"Girl broke." My mother laughed, insisting, "No."

A toddler, fanning grandpa, sickly pale,
I pray while holding his hand, beloved man
I spend each day with who, unlike my Dad,
Enjoys my company. When he goes limp,
Adults escort me out. "Gran needs me now!"
I scream. "He'd rather be alone," they lie.

A teen, adjusting wood Venetian blinds,
To see who's lighting fireworks, I spy guns
Inside a car as sirens suffocate
The peace. "I dated him," I told my Dad.
"Let the cops know!" He hissed, "You're mistaken."

Reality's uprooted, frankensteined
Into a dismal shape. My words became transformed,
Cassandra-like, provoking disbelief.
My truths remained green, stuck between my teeth.

How Pinch Kisses Ruined Me for Romance

Experiencing *pizzichilli* young —
All Neapolitan adults intent
On giving children sharp affection: kissed
With possibility of pain required —
I learned to squirm, becoming fruit, firm, ripe,
And ready to be pinched on shameless buds
Called cheeks.   Italians like operatic
Intensity: emotions leaving marks,
Or kisses raining fierce as cockpit bombs,
Assaults kids try escaping yet endure —
Young hearts confused from then, torn, victimized.

When do I live for opportunities
Like this? When do I duck? Always unsure,
Tattooed by *pizzichilli*, mind and soul
Re-enter fate's familiar feast of pain,
Know compromised enjoyment **must** be love.

Domus Pro Carcere

My kite is cornered. We want to get out
Where treetops wave. But Grandpa doesn't want
To fly or talk today. I can't ask why.

"Children are seen, not heard," my mother says,
"So shush!" She starts again in dialect fast,
The funny foreign language mother knows
That I don't understand. Gran won't explain
Because he says *Romano*'s, right, *bene* —
Correct Italian *principesse* speak
In fairytales he tells when I'm in bed,
That I first heard in English. I'm not sure
If they're the same girls who are rescued, freed,
Saved in Italian, like Rapunzella,
Shut up, her rope of blonde left long,
More than a kite's tail. I begged father not
To let them cut my hair. "I can't elope,"
I had explained. "How would my prince get in?"
He laughed at this and made me feel ashamed.

What's happening today? Three blackbirds screeched:
Unlucky sign. I rub my hunchback charm,
Then Grandpa's crucifix. He doesn't mind,
Stares off at something I can't see. Who's *this*?

A stranger with a suit and small black bag
Makes Grandma cry. But no one's chasing me,
So maybe it's okay. Our treetops wave.
"*Be'*! *Andiamo, nonno!*" I exclaim,
Moving my kite towards him not gripping back.
I wind myself back in, like pulling down
A winded kite. I've lost my ball of string,
I've somehow lost my way. My hair's too short,
Too dark for fairytales. Is this my fault?

Thoughts beat me back like evil birds of prey.
Odd heartbeats flush my ears, drown all my words.

A Little Choir Girl Contemplates Sin

Repent in Lent is what you do, transfixed
On misery, if you're good. I'm bad,
Kick-starting my imagination where
Angelic notes reside pitched higher than
My throat, where a humble alto's swept along
With a choir's gold harmonics, heaven sent
Sounds a family might make if charmed, music
Offering them another heart to eat.

In Brooklyn, spring pushed up loud daffodils.
Crab apples petaled roads as if to show
New marked (or safer) paths. Immaculate
Puffs grazing in the sky became lambs like
Agnus Dei, the sopranos poised for sins —
Peccata mundi — going up against
Determined steel: the organ pipes' lament.

Across the busy avenue, my schoolmate
Agnes is bouncing a ball to litanies
Rhymed, right leg up and under, her dress gay
As Easter eggs although it's Passiontide,
Devoted Tuesdays to the Sorrowful
Five Mysteries. I'm tempted — but no one's
Around to cross me. I'm returning late
From choir practice, rushing my errands
For mother, emptied from soap operas,
Competing with the Stations of the Cross.

That ball's pink, bouncy as my friend, all shorn
Now of our solemn school's drab uniform,
Some gold bit — locket maybe — on her neck,
Hung, swung like a target while she played today,
All unaware of me, my wave, blue eyes
Locked on the ball that's heading for traffic.

Conchshells, dead white, guard her front door, like ours,
Though nothing's the same inside. *Agnes!*
Why couldn't I be known for forgetting?

Sorrow tonight: meal's memory has stemmed
From *"Scourging at the Pillar,"*
Where Jesus, spotless, guiltless, is then beaten
For others' sins returns me to my oyster
Shell, hard home where I dwell with grains of sand,
Intruders I coat with a glaze to make their
Existence not so scratchy, making it
All easier to slip around till I'm good
And ready for that opening up. From
My curb, I can see over the hill where
A slope rose like a hunch, a humpback whale
Mid-block, fun to sled or bike over if
You dared, no grassy knoll this trellis-topped
Train trench, this urban hillside, its blank broken
Face blocking vehicles, cars gunning for
You with their solid metal presence in your
Immediate future, taking action
That could recast the universe in dark
Unpredictable ways. An oiltruck now
Is speeding, westbound, towards us, windshield coated
With weather, Agnes chasing her ball, bent
Low, smaller, in its path. All open my
Mouth, three notes rising — "God! Lord! Run!" — wired,
Unable to hold words in my mind, my
Prayer brittle as glass. Nothing lived in it.

No rescue. No child. "Your fault!" I can hear
My mother say. "What good are you?" I'm bad,
So useless, and invisible, in shock,
Observing Agnes, on the ground, mouth open,
Like mine, as a red cartoon balloon forms, and
A scream sat in my throat, raw, where I swallow,
Replaying the black revolution she
Took under such a fat front tire, ragdoll
In Easter pastels, virgin-martyr namesake
Saint Agnes slain at 12, an "older woman,"
Mature compared to us. A wave of people
Near her house closes off my view, adults
Who stood around before, all doing nothing,
Gape now for free and drown my sobs with buzzing,

Excited, empty. Two policemen write
On pads as a tall truck driver stands, head
In hands, like Jesus in "*The Agony in
The Garden*," thinking maybe of her or an
Abyss he glimpsed with no sweet remedy
Of light, azaleas swollen with potential
That Agnes never got to see. At home,
I'm speechless, normally, a hostage to
The dinners I eat to get rid of them. And,
Since Lent is fast and abstinence, there's pain's
Sad bouquet: pink and purple tentacles
On my plate, curving, curled like weapons. Dull
Dream daughter I become makes short cuts, clams
Up, pleading "mouth full!," Latin quiz tomorrow,
And bold strokes I'll unload on Saturday in
Confession as lies. Agnes is with our
Redeemer. If I were good, truly, I'd
Be comforted but I'm not, questions all
Suspended, too mysterious, tight roped
With sorry knowledge and memories ripe
As rotten cheese, my lost friend weaving through me
Like silk who met her dye. At bedtime, it's
A different dark waiting, grave, on-going
Sounds in my mind, truth tied up like a hobo
Sack I could run away with once, my private
Core ripped with wanting, having, not having.

    An innocent, dear Agnes, not like those
    Kicked early out of Paradise, always poised
    For trouble and braced for what's coming at us.

Custody Visit in the City of Angels

Sitting we wait for M-G-M Grand Air.

Sunglassed, that one's my father — but he's grown
A twin. One man gave me piggyback rides, named
Great stars in heaven, christened strange dustballs
Under my bed, making light of the dark,
Hugger called "dear Dadds," even when he left,
Went West to write. But shading reptile eyes:
Another guy my Mom's warned me about,
Who swears by bio-rhythms while angling
Development deals, praises re-hab groups.
"Poor women preyed on!" sniffs my aunt — pray *with*
Perhaps, since his hugs have gotten thinner.

Here, his "Whaddya want?" means *for dinner*.

What I want is to skip again, a hand
On either side. I'm tired of riots,
Goat cheese on food, not knowing who's used a bed.
His old apartment's nicer. Here police
Cruise in "a black and normal" and his friends
Seem so wild. Why is Angel skinny (if
Not "on meth" anymore)? There's Beth who needs
White mice because she keeps this snake. Dear Dadds
Must think he's Bogey: all I hear is "kid."

 "What's her sign?" — "Virgo, aren't you, kid?" What *is*
A grown-up doing with a python? It's
Called Gemini. Who cares if Cher's across
Our table? Tell me: what *is* that? I care about
This writer with no paper in his house,
No ribbons, stamps — then empties block his deck!

I wish he'd point at Pegasus's neck
Without that smell on his breath. *DADDS*! *Suggest
We BOTH walk through that gate*! No. His goodbye —
With shades on — is: "Don't mention Gemini."

Distorted Mirror

Because the other girls wore push-up bras
And Sweetie didn't, I got curious.
Instead of wearing low-cut denims that
Revealed a lacy thong, she chose full skirts.

Once in the cafeteria I ate
Too much and Sweetie demonstrated all
The various creative ways to purge,
Held my hair. "Better?" she asked. *OMG*!

That's how our friendship started — on empty.

"We're besties now!" I told my mother but
Omitting how those toothbrush tactics helped
Dislodge food. How we gorged on ice cream, cakes,
Pies, vomited together, side by side,
Like goddesses with sacred rituals,
Rewarded with a flatter stomach. Then
Snug pants seemed looser. Hipbones strutted out.

Eventually, toilets taunted me,
Bare tiles too painful for my bony knees.
I wore more layers, hid under wide skirts.

The male gaze, saturated sex and smirk,
Avoided us. Females were envious.

Soon Sweetie and I grew competitive.
Who could stop menstruating first? Who would
Lose more weight? She discovered laxatives,
Bragging that her commitment was total.

I fasted till I couldn't concentrate
In class, made lame excuses, anything
That might distract my teachers or buy time.

My weight caused incoherence. Friends weighed in,
Deciding who looked better, prettier,
More "runway fashion model" look-alike.
Few classmates voted for me. Sweetie won.

Physicians never spoke in English, used
Expressions they made up: "bulimia,"
"Body dysmorphia," "anorexic."

My Dad said "self-destructive." But my Mom,
Always dramatic, called it "a death wish."

This incoherence chewed me up, spat out
Illogical opinions, sickening,
Unhealthy, empty calorie theories
That only caused confusion and alarm.

Even before the toothbrush-toilet-thing
With Sweetie, honesty patrolled my room.

The moon-eyed courtyard of my cheval glass
Reflected on this, winked at me: *You're **fat**!*"

Stained Lass

Religion classes taught us to behave:
Defer fun's gratification. Submit.

The patriarchy ruled the afterlife —
Along with most improper things. Obliged.
Coerced. Imperfect those Confessions, stained.

Could any child prevent assaults or blab?

Each catechism lesson drilled down deep,
Swore death would be "the best day" of your life.

Meanwhile, your body was a sacrament,
Impure of thought and deed upon command.

Swift holy water dip on the way out.

Sticky Figs

Before I'm old enough to be some boy's
Intense, low-calorie, half innocent
Lip-smacking snack that leaves his young mouth wet
With decadent tastes, cravings that rock him
Awake, I learned to test a milky-sapped
Sac on its stem. Until it's ripe, you can't
Disturb a fig. Don't suck it, cradling
Its tender wrapper of unripened skin.

All winter, fig trees huddle under tarps,
Enjoying long pajama parties, stark
Naked, their branches tied, unable to stretch.

This hibernation — their adolescence —
Creates desired sweetness through its stem.

In autumn dried fruit decorates the plates,
Bright, wrinkled apricots, dark juicy figs,
Patience rewarded. With maturity
Comes knowing when to loot the tree — or wait.

Mermaid Lessons

Aromas like chlorine appealed to her.
Her therapist explained why pools feel safe:
Because she can avoid abusive men
While swimming. Chloe wants to answer "Duh!"

Instead she mounts the ladder, sees blue tiles —
Neat parallel lanes. Single file paths keep
Strange bodies separate, slow ones behind
Her swifter pace, one bathing cap per row.

As if in charge, she waits, clenched inward, till
A cobalt wand removes the obstacles,
Hosing the other bathers to the side.

In fantasy, her true self is revealed:
A deity — Olympian disguised.

She commandeers the springboard, muscles bunched,
Propelled, arms overhead. Jumps feel weightless
When she embraces the delectable
Pause at the peak, already in the first
Backward move — somersault — then gracefully
Beginning her next tumble, when she is
Aware her pimples, fat thighs, droopy breasts
Don't count, nor liquor bottles in the hall,
Mom's boyfriend with his sleazy grin, the puke
No one mops up, complaints about her grades.

The acqua world accepts her swanlike pose,
Glug gulps her down for a few moments then
She surfaces, glides towards the shallow end.

There is applause, though only she hears it.
Poseidon, her real father, would be proud.

Meanwhile, her therapist completed forms.
Emancipation's legalese and proofs —
Like earning money — are explained again.

"I'm never sure if you are listening.
Chloe, have you applied or interviewed?"

Omission is protection: the unsaid.
When family's as peaceful as riptide,
The game is rigged against a female child.

Escape, economize, and monetize.
That lifeguard opportunity will pay,
With extra income coaching divers, too.

How many swimmers on her watch will come
To *drown*, indulge the thrill of sinking down,
Awaiting sirens' funerary songs?

Familiar urge she knows — but now must thwart,
Arms arched, her mermaid tail attached, she dives,
Sleek swiftness under water, stronger willed,
Depriving strangers of their dreams of death,
And pounding chests till they decide to breathe.

She weighs the irony of rescuing,
That fate put *her* in charge of mermaid school.

Mother on Morphine

A madman crushed her favorite makeup
To paint my mother's floor. Imagine rouge
On top of powders, scattered door to door.
"I'll clean this up!" I say till she's relieved,
Obedient enough to swallow her
Tart, medicated, Lotos-like ice cream.
She's less combative, calmed by her morphine.
The mind's embrasures, freed from pain's embrace,
Will search for entertainment and escape
Confinement, longing to erase what's real.

Mom's traveling through Tinseltown and Rome
Of sixty years ago, a fond time when
Magnani commandeered "The Rose Tattoo."
Perhaps to mother films were fancy cures.
An audience suspected everything,
Eventually, would turn out just fine.
My mopping scrolls sweet fictions she can screen
Through fantasy, delaying hideous
Mortality, the final credits roll,
When shovels dance and dust returns to dust.

Since Roxanol has brought its soft hammer
To bear on mother's habit of rebuke,
We're playing she's an actress, which helps script
Reality. A Brooklyn closet is
"A dressing room," her home "a trailer" parked
Aside the set. She's idle now because
It's needed — her director will demand
That shot where she looks rested. It's agreed
She'll close her eyes while I beat grief from rugs.

Making a comeback, newly patient, she
Rehearses. It's an unfamiliar role,
With gentle words expressed with self-control,
Extending herself to unseen marquees.

Detecting flickers of excitement keyed
By movie light, I hope there's room for me.

When Fathers Disappear

When fathers disappear, they take their name —
Along with the certainty they loved those who
Were left behind, deserted. Families
Can overwinter, silent, wondering.

Perhaps his name was fake, an alias.

Deceptive Dads erase all memories:
Cold righteous looks, prophetic sighs, door slams.
He'd been a mouthpiece, a provider once.
Imaginative words, incisive wit
Will introduce himself to women's eyes,
Who'll see potential, dream's aristocrat,
Misreading his moods for profundity.

All unaware, one blindly takes him in.

Compliance has its price, which makes him twitch,
Then adumbrate new plans each time he shaves.

When gearshifts of a train have more appeal
Than bottomless parental collar-grabs,
He'll leave for cigarettes and not return —
Nor face those bad names touching everything.

Romance Attacks My Dance Card

The thunder polka of a new romance
Began today on my left foot, the one
Believed to lead suggestiveness astray.

True love's a waltz: it's measured and mature
Like patience set to action. Dance decodes
The blood, translates the shadows of the soul,
Emotions dipping, swelling at the door
Called "sense." Romance corsaged my heart and wrists
Again. Will filled my dance card out because
That blinding barrier shores up dreamwork.
Hopes rubbed together. Sanity, once my
Sly chaperone, no longer is with us.

Duty at Mekong Delta

They're white as rice that wasn't thrown at us.
His stack of letters (nineteen-sixty-eight's
Mail, barely legible) was saved, penned straight,
Not far from enemy lines. Infamous:
The Mekong Delta, toured by curious
Loved ones, prepared to demonstrate
Our grief, disarm now, do what liberates,
Surrendering to the incongruous.

His presence here seems reconstructed as
Those letters fold my world to paper wings.
Why do brave words demand laments? I meant
To re-read, gather them for warmth — whereas
I light a match, red breast flames releasing
Angels illegible in their ascent.

A Vine Affair

He was a cabernet: his type could grow
Wild anywhere and thrive despite being
Neglected. She was a pinot: clinging,
Thin-skinned and temperamental, yielding though
In need of constant care. In bed this beau
Rolled her around, felt her on his tongue. King
Of Hefner's creed, he sniffed, sipped, savoring,
Tasting. She wore an imbecilic glow.

This pinot came alive, drove blood pressure
Up, thus she gained complexity until
That typical, inevitable mad
Decline. He's ready for a French wine tour.
She's ordering depresso, taking pills.
He dreams of zin — vim that's Olympiad.

The Milliner's Late Night

Her millinery shop had windows bright
With fascinators for madame whose face
Needs artificial lace to help erase
Ten years and homburgs for suburbanites
Disguised as understated socialites.
She scanned the sawdust-trampled street in case
Her customer was late or had misplaced
The payment for this bretonne veiled in white.

Winds cold as fingers of an old cashier
Blew scraps through the boutique as beggars took
Their place. The organ grinder's monkey held
His fez when coins appeared as sunset neared.
A lady, cloaked, knocked with a frantic look
As, in the distance, wedding steeples belled.

Run-Away Bride — or The Mermaid's Lament

Bree made a wish inspired by broke girls
In fairytales, not realizing then
Mist magic isn't free. Before smoke curled
For dinnertime, she quit the sea for him.

Her human limbs are pale, not powerful
Like mermaids' tails. They can't kick hard enough,
Return Bree to the deep blue beautiful
Realm underwater, force that made her tough.

Their wedding lullabied anxiety
Away. Then moods wrecked her loveboat. And she'd
Draw baths, avoiding his society
To sink beneath, imagining seaweed,
That salt encrusted skin, fins, cool order
She'd dreamt of giving up. He built their pool.
The shoals and eddies of chlorined waters
Are hers to rule now, cruelly fooled.

Cedar Waxwings

My youngest sister's dying first. That's not
How it's supposed to be — thoughts I push hard,
Harder, the small soprano in the swing
Flying to greet the blue with her high C.

She has her mother's eyes, and begs for more
With promises she *will hold on!* — a good girl
Who's never-never-bound. Soon she won't fit
In this contraption, chubby legs too close
Already to the frame. I've just explained:
Some things grow fast like cedars — massing thick
Enough to matter, so strong they repel
Most other forces. High above us now
Cedars shield us from wind, block the cold rooms
Where promise grows, exposing flesh closer
To bones, a chest without hope, a matter
Of time. Trees near this playground stir, newborn.

Swift cedar waxwings bring their young treats, greet
A vast horizon, optimistic might,
As I try pushing so much weight away.

   A girl on a swing, returns to me, again, again,
   Protected, safe, and saved. *Hold on, my love. Hold on!*

Embodiment

My sister lives forever in six drawers
Where Mom maintains her clothing, worn, outgrown.

Preserved in cameras, she's chambered,
Sealed shut like darkroom prints, unmoving face
Still undeveloped as her unspent youth.

Moored on his island of bad memories,
Her boyfriend, claiming self-defense, wears stripes.

Nighttime she's back, soft stabled in seizures
Of stars or hovering in ghost orb's mist.

A pinch of lonely air lifts blankets, hugs
Half of my bedding. No heat radiates.

The younger person I still am inside
Peers out. Instead of ghost dents on the sheets,
I see her shuffling the deck, smell smoke
From phantom joints, red lipsticked, decayed dreams
Beyond my line of sight, time's taut trapeze.

I yearn to grab her wrist, yank heart and soul
From cold oblivion, yell, "Breathe again!"
Hope hops on life support, prepared to drag
Her from the brink and storm the underworld.

Geometry's shades fade — by dawn's dispersed.

The Suicide Surrogate Confesses

Perhaps she wished to mimic opera's
Iconic heroines, envisioning
This love as indispensable yet doomed.

Tonight he called, insisting he'll commit
To it. He'll kill himself — he really will.
As usual, she was encouraging.

Then he had second thoughts. He couldn't breathe
The toxic fumes. Why not phone the police?
Or notify his family? Instead
She argued with him, "Get back in the truck!"

Obeying her commands, his body wrapped
Around the nameless weight his life became,
Afraid no longer of its siren song.

His absence filled his parents' painbrain, torched
Those memories of suicide attempts.
His girlfriend took his life away from them.

Demanding justice, they watched screens replay
Text messages debating the ideal
Method for dating death successfully.

"Sorry I let you do this," she confessed.

After the verdict's read, the gavel pounds
The desk for order — and lifts satisfied.

Note: The suicide of Conrad Henri Roy III [1995—2014], with encouragement from his long-distance girlfriend, Michelle Carter, 17, was the subject of a noted investigation and involuntary manslaughter trial in Bristol County, Massachusetts, known as the "texting suicide case."

The Bridge Crossing

Suicidal dreams suspend questions of the night. Saudi sisters adrift in New York, darkness rowing them to sinister emirates. Penniless. Sorrow transported them to a souk where they barter, trading hunger for another afternoon in America. Fraught memories they finger like worry beads. A close-mouthed sky spits on the indigent. Dirty pigeons point to the river. They've become feathers, light in the arms of kismet.

> gold and copper foliage release
> the brittle branch with a whispered sigh
> floating to meet the earth's
> patchwork carpet
> their fate fulfilled

Staten Island Ferry. Accusing north winds whip open coats like a Customs Officer. The sixteen-year-old sister imagines gliding through the tide of clasped hands to a safe haven. Liberty's torch reminds the twenty-three-year-old sister of Aladdin's lamp, a jinni armed with wishes. Then a breeze strips a discarded sandwich of its wrapper. Like terns, these two foreigners scavenge for crusts. Ahead seagulls forage for food, squawking rude reminders like impertinent desk clerks.

> catching sight
> of bleary-eyed reflections
> in the hotel's cheval glass
> they forgot
> the emptiness beneath

Central Park. Facing east, they perform *Salah*. Women walk dogs, shiny dark hair free as a raven's wings, legs bare unlike daughters of their desert homeland, always petitioning men for assent. Decisions will fly tonight, inked on postcards, explaining why return is impossible. Manhattan's mud-tinged sky is brightening to blue. They walk uptown, guided by the path of Bow Bridge as ducks quack complaints. *Still here?*

> doves nesting
> at the lake's edge
> knitting a new home
> out of trash
> and exhausted leaves

George Washington Bridge. Unadorned steel. A domesticated red lighthouse squats at its base not unlike crusaders' tombs, faithful stone pets guarding the foot. Warm weather wrestles with their heavy coats, rocks buried in pockets. Makeshift shrouds. Winds stir undependable shadows as they ascend, dare nervous legs to reach a high ledge. A dramatic draping is left to the older sibling. Consigning their sisterhood to the pledge of duct-tape, they jump in tandem. Submerged and gone, momentary mermaids, their mighty splash a proclamation.

> boats glide over swells
> dusk darkening the Hudson River
> waves rolling off their backs
> late autumn chill gathering power
> approaching day of the dead

Note: Saudi sisters Rotana Farea, 23, and Tala Farea, 16, were found on the rocky banks of the Hudson River, duct-taped to each other. Bound together, they had jumped off the George Washington Bridge. Police discovered their bodies on October 24, 2018.

Footprints in the Snow

It's the same dream. It wakes me up each time.
Could it be some ghost family returned?

Asleep, strange shards of memory poke me
Like spikes. The walls are melancholy now
Since she slipped out that winter, calloused feet
Shoeless although it snowed for hours. Chills
Came creeping into corners by the stove
And stood behind me when I held a knife.

My neighbors said police checked mental wards,
All accident reports, and combed the woods.

They found no trace. Her husband sold the house.

Neglected properties need TLC,
Attract those good at caretaking. It's strange
Quiet arrives in sudden blasts of cold,
Announcing it resists all ownership.

I don't recognize my own fireplace.
Who cut this cord of wood, left embers, ash
Inside the pit? When I bend to smooth sheets,
I sense cool whispering. The window shines,
Reveals it snowed tonight and left fresh prints,
Small, delicate. The person was barefoot.

I am afraid to be responsible,
Afraid to be asked questions. Please, stay away.

The Lady of the Dunes: A Cold Case

In 1974 on Cape Cod,
That harsh assaulting song of gulls masked screams.
Long red hair placed on a bandanna, jeans,
Nude body on a towel, looking odd,
Both hands removed, jaw open as if sawed
By killers who pulled teeth, destroyed the means
Of learning her identity and cleaned
The crime scene. Now she's only known to God.

No missing person's report. No one sought
To claim or bury her. There was no sign
Nor clues that someone witnessed her demise.
Her mutilated corpse lay in the morgue,
Anonymously sealed in its cold shrine.
Justice is those monks chanting for her rise.

Note: "Lady of the Dunes" is the nickname for an unidentified woman discovered on July 26, 1974 in the Race Point Dunes, Provincetown, Massachusetts. Her murder remains unsolved.

A Ghost Revisits a Tattoo Parlor

Like marriage, this will hurt, a sacrament
That marks flesh, inks and needles, an array
Of patterns, birds, begonias, names entwined.

Observing his new bride, examining
Marmoreal fresh skin, I'm noticing
Three hickies on her neck, love's artifacts.

His rage, suppressed for now, will take that throat,
Stain it with thumbprints, purple necklaces
Requiring camouflage — scarves, turtlenecks.

Inside a heart, the artist carefully
Inks her beloved's name, an alphabet
Of dark regrets, as if she'll be unmoored
Without this simulacrum. Ownership
Of permanent I.D. — tattoos, birthmarks —
Is useful when cops find a battered corpse,
Need ghostly guides, a name tag for the morgue.

Little Towel Thieves

When had she settled for impermanence
Called other-woman-hood? Affairs had no
Build to them, frail foundations spun thought-sewn
From sugar — a shady borrowed residence.

His wife will never give him a divorce,
Unless the stars align, he likes to say.
Compliance and deceit can't pave love's way.
Contacting Mrs. X was one recourse.

The hope chest she'd inherited (a tableau
Of joyful possibilities) accused
A faith fed by bad intentions. What excused
Her for sustaining a wrongful status quo?

Driving to meet his wife, her prologue spins,
Rehearsing. Shouldn't she apologize?
Some poplars groomed a lesson in disguise:
Like sheltering trees, marriage broke the wind

At a couple's back. Attention cultivates
Roots — not this daze of stolen interludes.
Approaching his house (their home) inner feuds
Pause when she sees a group of children: eight

Sweet little girls in heels played "dressing up."
One swipes white towels from a clothesline. Friends
Affix this bridal veil and Mendelssohn
Her down imaginary aisles, disrupt

Roses — a shower acted out in mime.
The little towel thieves then flee, disperse
Before the laundress sees linen coerced
Into their crime, abandoned, left behind.

Returning home, hands shift into neutral,
Orderly trees receding. Boundaries
Are blurred. Red petals meet the breeze that frees
Them. Night falls on retired rituals.

Valentine's Villanelle

Although I've made it holy in my mind —
Our sweet hypnotic love, my fantasy —
That place I left by your side was not mine.

Confounding me with sounds my heart refined,
Unsteady dreaming fanned hyperbole.
(Instead I've made it holy.) In my mind,

Stored, polished memories of us still shine,
Attaching me to what was not to be.
That place I left by your side wasn't mine.

Love's air is thin. Love's words breathe hard, designed
To signify rich unreality —
As though I've made it wholly in my mind.

She drinks you dry, so here you are, inclined
Towards me, embracing chance illegally.
That place I left by your side wasn't mine.

My parents named me for Saint Valentine.
A martyr's passion is his ecstasy.
But though I've made you holy in my mind,
That place I left by your side wasn't mine.

Merchants of Venus

I'm dreaming Venice is inclined towards us.
Reality is not that likable.
My city here is warring with itself.
Your city there contains your awful wife.

It's *my* dream, so I've picked Venezia,
Inclined towards us, its nighttime waves uncoiled,
Restricting no one, pathless, lapping sea
To stones. Forget the official version
Of our unquiet love. This dream stars me
Parading in my slip — Venetian-laced
Like my communion dress, white altar-wear.
Desiring to distraction, I watch you,
My priest of love, black-robed and bearing down
On me, expecting that I'll open wide
For what, my host in Venice, I've been told
My teeth are not supposed to touch.   Affairs,
It seems, teach you to swallow; pride goes first,
Then other things. I learned, my mouth secured,
Kiss-tied, arms fastened — holding, letting go,
Restricting no one. Wet words lapped us up.
You put the taste for dark clouds in my mouth,
And waves in both hands. You walked on water.
You still do, ruling this, the bubbling world.
My willow soul seeks moisture under dirt
Through open holes in heart's halls, sucking you
Into my pungent labyrinth, content,
Moving in love's gyration dance, absorbed.

High on the oars of feeling, joy comes, lasts.

All bridges are suspended near my home,
Where I'm at war with my untoward life,
Painting — not Turner's Venice, light let loose,
A pious town tipped with paired steeples, belled —
Instead a quiet crawl alongside you,
Bearer of unattainable aged dreams,
On this black canvas of estrangement, not
Part of your city where rains come hard, not
Half of a damaged marriage — *still* employed
By Lawfirm Love, where we're secret partners.

The Wake

The funeral's assemblage — standing room
Full — humid honeycomb of black-winged veils
Amid a lone queen bee who, rumors say,
Is now quite wealthy, stared as the young priest
Recalled the life of the deceased, a man
He never met. In air arranged by gnats,
This widow might feel the scourge of jealousy
Of wasp-waisted blonde mistresses who sought
The secret bin of sweetness avidly
But dreamt a better end to this affair.

Anonymous bouquets surround his bier.
All roses have been shorn of thorns as if
Transgressive floral displays might cause tears
Throughout the endless swarm from honey-house.

An accidental overdose occurred
Before her husband could file for divorce
As planned. Conspicuously, her eyes close
While mourners pray or check their buzzing phones.

Her mind is cataloguing shameful stings
Of infidelity. Son of a b.

My Dungeon Ghost

"If ye will listen to me, but for a little while, I will tell it … in story stiff and strong…"
— Gawain and the Green Knight

I.

He gave me my first kiss, a kiss which all
Others aspire to be. But that was not
As memorable as when he crept up
Behind me, deep in the stacks with Shakespeare,
And thrust *Le Morte d'Arthur* into my life.

Uther Pendragon, Lady of the Lake,
La Belle Isolde, Lamorak, Galahad,
Gawain and the Green Knight: he'd rattle off
These names like boys on our block recited
Today's New York Yankees' starting line-up.

Under his spell, I became capable
Of sin, adulteress wed to the head
Of Camelot, while disreputably
Cavorting. He cast me as Guinevere,
Himself as Lancelot, my illicit
Paramour. Troubadours lionized my
Beauty. Fortified by my favor, he
Won all tournaments, adoring his new
Heroic entity, the prison-like
Grip of its shallowness, his eyes askew.

Fantasy twitched, hid its murderous heart.

We're library-eyed sixth graders, bewitched
By British poetry, legends, and lore.
He's eleven years old. I'd just turned nine.

Sundays we'd serve God together, speaking
Liturgical Latin, prim altar boy
In the sanctuary, his Juliet
On the balcony — choir loft — voice raised.
"Lead us not into temptation," we'd sing.

In class we'd pass naughty notes, wild words penned
By Malory, Tennyson, and Chaucer.
He dreamt of noble crusades, mighty steeds.
I thought about what constitutes the light
'Round which friends gather, pull each other up.

Three years later, I cast aside wimples,
Tippets, and my power to petition,
As Camelot's queen, for a Papal Bull.

The Round Table was no more, upended.
Graduation. New unknowns descended.

II.

   "Sir Knight, if thou cravest battle here thou shalt not fail for lack of a foe."

There he was on horseback at The Cloisters,
Preparing to joust, taller, brawnier,
More Green Knight than Gawain but, all the same,
A *verray, parfit, gentil knyght*. No words
Passed. *His baner desplayeth, and forth rood.*

When I described his armor to neighbors,
They derided him: college drop-out, drunk,
An unseemly Port Authority cop.

*"Knight or patrolman, he's a barrier
To chaos. Love whatever saves your life!"*
This sassed retort is thought, not said. What nerve.
My words have more heft than gossips deserved.

Instead I kept my fingers on the pulse
Of Chaucer, Tennyson, Malory, Bede,
Chretien de Troyes, and William Langland,
Earned my degrees by forgetting to sleep,
Becoming an anchoress, books knee deep.

III.

Decades passed. When his voice returned, as if
Magnetic force spun a dusty mix-tape
From life's forgotten hits, as if he'd reeled
Me back to the library's Children's Room,
As if he were transmitting from the spheres,
I was too busy to listen at first.

When his voice returned, insistent, troubled,
It took three weeks before his confession
Was complete. His crimes were unspeakable,
Impressed their brutish force across the miles.

During the course of a contract murder,
His cowardice left an infant to starve,
Bawling inside her crib, though her father
Made provisions for her safe retrieval
From this house of carnage. But the killers —
Two men who'd sired children — did not phone.

In air arranged by bees, the final sting
Blitzed: a slow-witted male was convicted,
Stewed behind bars for nine years, innocent,
Incapable of such a heinous crime,
While my friend refused to speak, let it be,
Abused his liberty by offering
Himself as a paid assassin for hire.

Sweet altar boy, who rang the bells during
Lent's *Miserere*, had turned mercenary.

Arrests came ten years later when he was
Outed. His partner, ill now, suddenly
Decided to name the victim's husband
And him, betraying his accomplices.

Hours spent with the venerable Bede
Enlightened us to the ways of the world,
Its fickleness and instability.
We valued courtly love and *curteisie.*

What incited moral degradation?

"Ye gan to grucche me!" was his sore complaint.
Yet he explained how he sought false glory,
A mad pursuit of titles — duke and king —
Jousting in a mirrored colosseum,
Betraying himself, forever in debt.

Consumed by shallowness, pride, and regret,
My friend had declined a coherent eye.

To offer him cash, I phoned the prison.

"He's been gone a month," the chaplain advised.
"When no one claimed him, inmates dug his grave."

"Prithee grant an inestimable boon,
My queen, whose loyalty's my only hope.
Family hates me but find my daughter.
Say I'm very sorry and I love her."

I thought of what the Green Knight told Gawain:
Kindness, mercy, and what's "less than to blame."
I pledged fealty. Then he said her name.

> *A knyght ther was and that a worthy man,*
> *That fro the tyme that he first bigan*
> *To riden out, he loved chivalrie,*
> *Trouthe and honour, fredom and curteisie.*

Notes: Section headings are all from *Gawain and the Green Knight*.
"verray, parfit…"   Chaucer, *The Canterbury Tales*, *General Prologue*,
            line 72
"His baner desplayath…" Chaucer, *The Knight's Tale*, line 966
"A knyght ther was…"   Chaucer, *The Canterbury Tales*, *General Prologue*,
            lines 43-46

The Subway Pervert

Because all dirty crimes we can't unsee
Are kept by brain's biographer, replayed,
The Subway Pervert cannot be erased.

As if by previous arrangement, he'd
Be waiting after class — ten forty-five
PM — his cock unleashed on subway stairs
While masturbating, daring passersby
To stare or stop his public pleasuring.

He blocked the only entrance to my train.

Ignoring him, determined to get past
Untouched — this tollbooth troll outwitted me.
He knew disgust and fear exact their fees.

Women's untold lives are controlled, fish-bowled —
Cat-calling from construction crews, roughed up
By roofies, rubbed the wrong way by frotteurs,
Man-handled by suspicious fiancés —
As hot male breath clouds up once clear water.

I fantasize about invisible
Shields — safe greenhouses with protective glass
For goddesses who'll never be defiled.

LindaAnn LoSchiavo

Native New Yorker LindaAnn LoSchiavo, a Pushcart Prize, Rhysling Award and Dwarf Stars nominee, is a member of the Science Fiction Poetry Association and The Dramatists Guild of America.

Elgin Award winner "A Route Obscure and Lonely" and "Concupiscent Consumption" are her latest poetry titles.

Forthcoming: a full-length poetry collection by Beacon Books as well as an illustrated collaborative chapbook devoted to Hallowe'en, "Messengers of the Macabre," co-written with David Davies.

She has been leading a poetry critique group for two years.

Her Texas Guinan documentary won "Best Feature Documentary" at N.Y. Women's Film Fest (Dec. 2021).

https://linktr.ee/LindaAnn.LoSchiavo

Twitter: @Mae_Westside

LindaAnn Literary on YouTube:
https://www.youtube.com/channel/UCHm1NZIlTZybLTFA44wwdfg.

Acknowledgements

How Pinch Kisses Ruined Me for Romance
      — in *Mused, Bella Online Literary Review*

Domus Pro Carcere
      — in *The Poet Magazine*; rpt in *Pure Slush Books* (Australia)

A Little Choir Girl Contemplates Sin
      — in *tnr* [as "Agnus Dei']; winner of the *tnr's* 3rd Poetry Award

Custody Visit in the City of Angels
      — in *WildSound Poetry Festival* [as "Visiting Gemini"]; & won a PEN contest

Distorted Mirror
      — in *CERASUS Magazine* (U.K.)

Stained Lass
      — in *The Cabinet of Heed*; rpt in *Blood and Bourbon* (Canada)

Sticky Figs
      — in *Swim Press* (U.K.)

Mother on Morphine
      — in *Wax Poetry and Arts*; 2nd Prize Winner; rpt in *World's Best Poems, Vol. 1*

When Fathers Disappear
      — in *Peregrine Journal*

Romance Attacks My Dance Card
      — in *Peacock Journal*

Duty at Mekong Delta
      — in *PIF*

The Milliner's Late Night
      — in *Not Very Quiet* (Australia)

Runaway Bride or The Mermaid's Lament
— in *The Gambler*

Cedar Waxwings
— in *Measure*

Embodiment
— in *The Healing Muse*; rpt in *The BeZine*

The Suicide Surrogate Confesses
— in *Pennsylvania Literary Journal*

The Bridge Crossing
— in *Drifting Sands Haibun*

Footprints in the Snow
— in *Panoplyzine*; & won a contest sponsored by *F(r)iction*

The Lady of the Dunes: A Cold Case
— in *A Portrait of New England*

A Ghost Revisits a Tattoo Parlor
— in *Gravitas* (Canada)

Little Towel Thieves
— in *The Bacon Review*

Merchants of Venus
— in *Eros, An Anthology of Poetry and Prose* [Robin Barratt, Editor]

The Wake
— in *Red Wolf Journal* (Singapore)

My Dungeon Ghost
— in *The-504*

The Subway Pervert
— in Indolent Books, *What Rough Beast* series